Mia Discovers

ROME

by Alexandria Pereira

AuthorHouse™
1663 Liberty Drive
Bloomington, IN 47403
www.authorhouse.com
Phone: 833-262-8899

This book is printed on acid-free paper.

ISBN: 978-1-6655-4427-6 (sc)
ISBN: 978-1-6655-4426-9 (hc)
ISBN: 978-1-6655-4428-3 (e)

Library of Congress Control Number: 2021923147

Print information available on the last page.

Published by AuthorHouse 11/15/2021

authorHOUSE®

The Mystery of History Series
Book 3 of 4

Dedication

To my grandma - for her constant encouragement, wisdom and love.

"This lunch is good, Grandma," said Mia.

"Thank you. What would you like to do after lunch?" said Grandma.

"Could we go to the museum again? I want to learn about Romans," said Mia.

"That sounds like a great idea. Let's visit the museum today and learn about our Roman history," said Grandma.

"Grandma, who are these people?" Mia asked.

"These people are the Etruscans. They came after our Neanderthal ancestors many, many, thousands of years ago," said Grandma, carefully sounding out *Uh*-truh-*sknz*. "The Etruscans started our big cities like Rome and Florence," said Grandma.

Bust of Juno
380 B.C.

truscan Bust
3rd Century B.C.

"And these people, Grandma?" Mia asked.

"These people are the Greeks. They sailed to Italy from the country called Greece. They brought great ideas for building things, and ways to read and write," said Grandma.

Bust of Dionysis
138 A.D.

"Oh, Grandma, I know who these people were! They were the Romans," said Mia.

"Yes, these are the Romans. The Etruscans and Greeks taught the Romans how to build things. They also taught the Romans the alphabet, and how to make foods like pizza and ice cream.

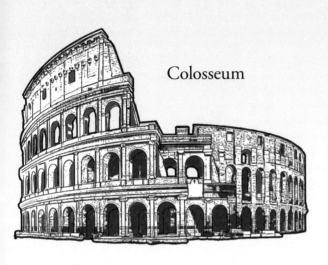

Colosseum

Pantheon

"The Romans then built many more things. The Colosseum is a huge amphitheater similar to today's sporting arenas. Aqueducts carried water to Rome from far away. The Pantheon is so wonderful that many copies of it have been built around the world. The Romans built many, many roads, from Rome to almost everywhere they traveled.

Aqueduct

"Oh, Mia, I'm getting tired. Could we go home now?" said Grandma.

"Could we please stay just a little longer? I really want to know more. Could we get a snack and keep going?" said Mia.

"OK. While we eat our snack, would you like to know some more cool things about Rome?" said Grandma.

"Yes," said Mia.

"Do you like volcanoes?" Grandma asked.

"Yes, they are super cool," said Mia.

"Well, during Roman times, the Mount Vesuvius volcano erupted. A lot of ash and lava came out of the volcano and covered the towns of Pompeii and Herculaneum. Centuries later, Mount Vesuvius erupted again. I was a child then. Since cameras had been invented, a pilot was able to take a picture of the volcano as he was flying near it, and I saw that picture in the newspaper. Some of the ash even reached the City of Rome," said Grandma.

"Wow!" said Mia.

"Here's another cool thing. Did you know that inside the City of Rome there is a whole other country? It is called the Vatican. Rome is the only city in the world to have another country inside it. The Vatican has its own government and rules, and all the people work together. It is also the smallest country in the world," said Grandma.

"That is super cool, Grandma!" said Mia.

"Done with your snack?" said Grandma.

"Yup," said Mia.

"Then let's finish our history about Rome.

"As more and more people were born, they started to have arguments with one another. To try and get along, the people made a government where they could make rules together. They called this government the Roman Republic. Then many years later, one man decided that he wanted to make all the rules himself. His name was Julius Caesar. He made a lot of new rules, and people did not like them. People in the government told him no and made a new government without him called the Roman Empire. The Roman Empire lasted for over one thousand years, and let its people help make the rules.

"Now eventually the Roman Empire ended, and so did its government and laws. The people now needed a new way to solve their problems. By working together, they made new rules and a new government. They called this new government the Kingdom of Italy. Later the people decided to call their government the Italian Republic, and all the people lived together in the country of Italy," said Grandma.

"I can see all the changes my family made over so many years so that I could be here today. I'm glad I live in a place with such fun things to learn. I wonder what I can do to help my Italian family work together to solve problems and improve on rules and government? My history is no longer a mystery. I live in Italy, and this was my and Rome's history. Thank you, Grandma," said Mia.

"You are welcome," said Grandma.

Historical Timeline

800 BC	The Etruscans start populating Italy. Iron is used for the first time.
753	Romans first appear in Italy.
700	Greeks start populating parts of southern Italy.
509	The Roman Republic is founded.
45	Julius Caesar becomes ruler of Rome.
44	Julius Caesar's rule ends.
27	Augustus becomes the first emperor of the Roman Empire.
79 AD	Mount Vesuvius erupts, covering the towns of Pompeii and Herculaneum.
80	Construction of the Roman Colosseum is completed.
128	The Roman Pantheon built by Emperor Hadrian.
147	The Roman Empire starts to fall.
395	The Roman Empire splits into two halves. The Western half is ruled from Rome.
476	End of the Western half of the Roman Empire.
800	Charlemagne is crowned the leader of the new Holy Roman Empire.
1498	Michelangelo sculpts the *Pietà*, located in the Vatican.
1508	Michelangelo begins painting the ceiling of the Sistine Chapel in the Vatican.
1861	The Kingdom of Italy is formed.
1871	Rome joins Kingdom of Italy and is named its capital.
1929	The Vatican, or Holy See, becomes its own country within the city of Rome.
1944	Mount Vesuvius erupts again on March 18.
1946	The Italian Republic is formed.
1999	Italy joins the European Union as one of six founding members.

Education Support Activities

Basic Human Needs

food
shelter
clothing
the need to socialize
the need to solve problems, invent, and be
creative

Practical Life and Sensorial Foundation

Engage children in activities characteristic of
Italy
plant a seed
wash grapes
sweep outside steps or walkway
hang cloths on a clothes line

History

past, present, and future
timelines

Science

innovation
building and engineering

Geography and Map Work

continents
Europe
significant landforms

Botany

focus on grapes and other agricultural products
of Italy

Earth Science

volcanoes

Peace Curriculum

peace table process
conflict resolution skills

Printed in the United States
by Baker & Taylor Publisher Services